The Art of Cricket 2009

Yearbook and Desk Diary

original paintings by

Christina Pierce

Best Wishes Christina Pierce

Published by Christina Pierce in association with
Dodo Pad Ltd. PO Box 33, St. Agnes, Cornwall TR5 0WU

Design and Produced by Mick Hodson Associates

Original Concept & Illustrations © Christina Pierce 2008

ISBN 978 1 903001 547

ISBN 978 1 903001 554 (100 signed copies by the artist)

Printed in Thailand

Contents

For my parents
David and Jean Pierce

County Clubs

01332 388 101	Derbyshire (1870)	County Ground, Grandstand Road, Derby DE21 6AF
0191 387 1717	Durham (1882)	County Ground, Riverside, Chester-le-Street, Co. Durham DH3 3QR
01245 252420	Essex (1876)	County Ford Ground, New Writtle Street, Chelmsford, Essex CM12 0PG
0871 282 3401	Glamorgan (1888)	SWALEC Stadium, Cardiff CF11 9XR
0117 910 8000	Gloucestershire (1870)	The County Ground, Nevil Road, Bristol BS7 9EJ
0238047 2002	Hampshire (1863)	The Rose Bowl, Botley Road, West End, Southampton SO30 3XH
01227 456 886	Kent (1859)	St Lawrence Ground, Old Dover Road, Canterbury, Kent CT1 3NZ
0161 282 4000	Lancashire (1864)	Old Trafford, Manchester M16 0PX
0116 283 2128	Leicestershire (1879)	County Ground, Grace Road, Leicester LE2 8AD
020 7289 1300	Middlesex (1864)	Lord's Cricket Ground, London NW8 8QN
01604 514 455	Northamptonshire (1878)	County Ground, Abington Avenue, Northampton NN1 4PR
0115 982 3000	Nottinghamshire (1838)	Trent Bridge, Nottingham NG2 6AG
0845 337 1875	Somerset (1875)	County Ground, St James Street, Taunton, Somerset TA1 1jT
08712 461 100	Surrey (1845)	The Brit Insurance Oval, Kennington, London SE11 5SS
0844 264 0202	Sussex (1839)	County Ground, Eaton Road, Hove, Sussex BN3 3AN
0870 062 1902	Warwickshire (1882)	County Ground, Edgbaston, Birmingham B5 7QU
01905 748 474	Worcestershire (1865)	County Ground, New Road, Worcester WR2 4QQ
0113 278 7394	Yorkshire (1863)	Headingley Cricket Ground, Leeds LS6 3BU

Derbyshire County Cricket Club

County Ground

Address: Grandstand Road, Derby, DE21 6AF

E mail: info@derbyshireccc.com

Main telephone number: 01332 388 101

Web site address: www.derbyshireccc.com

Ticket Sales:
01332 388 101
sue.evans@derbyshireccc.com

Press / Media Enquiries:
Tom Holdcroft, 01332 388 125
tom.holdcroft@derbyshireccc.com

Match Day Catering:
01332 388 119
abbie.gray@derbyshireccc.com

Meetings and Events:
01332 388 105
crissi.akers@derbyshireccc.com

Hospitality / Corporate Bookings:
01332 388 107
kerry.madeley@derbyshireccc.com

Shop:
01332 388 101
sue.evans@derbyshireccc.com

Online Shop:
www.derbyshireccc.com

Minor County Grounds:
Chesterfield

Officials

Chief Executive:
Tom Sears, 01332 388 103
tom.sears@derbyshireccc.com

Chairman:
Don Amott

Honorary Secretary:
David Griffin

Head of Cricket:
John Morris
john.morris@derbyshireccc.com

Captain:
Rikki Clarke

Groundsman:
Neil Godrich, neil.godrich@derbyshireccc.com

Membership Department:
Sue Evans, 01332 388 101
sue.evans@derbyshireccc.com

Benefit Year:
Stephen Stubbings

Travel Information:

From M1 South: Take exit 25 - A52 Derby. After 6 miles arrive at PENTAGON ISLAND. The ground is 4th exit off this roundabout, signposted with a brown cricket sign.

From M1 North: Take exit 28 - A38 Derby. After approx 13 miles, arrive at roundabout, take 1st exit A61, signposted with a brown cricket sign. Follow over 2 more roundabouts, stay on A61. Just before 3rd roundabout, PENTAGON ISLAND, take left turn into cricket ground. If you should miss it, take 1st exit off roundabout into ground.

From Birmingham: Travel up A38 to A61 roundabout. Take 2nd exit, A61 Derby signposted with a brown cricket sign. Follow over 2 more roundabouts, PENTAGON ISLAND, take left turn into cricket ground, if you should miss it, take 1st exit off roundabout into ground.

From M6: Take exit, J15 (from south), J16 (from north), follow signs to A50 (Uttoxeter). Follow A50 approx 20 miles to A516 to Derby. Take A516 until it joins A38 then follow directions (from Birmingham) above

Derbyshire County Cricket Club

County Cricket

Derbyshire Cricket Board
www.dcbcricket.com

County Youth Development:
Chris Porter, 01332 388 131
chris.porter@derbyshireccc.com

Emerging Players Coach:
Howard Dytham, 01332 388 131
howard.dytham@derbyshireccc.com

Cricket Board Administrator:
Jacqui Hall, 01332 388 111
jacqui.hall@derbyshireccc.com

Women's Cricket Co-ordinator:
Greig Wright, 07791 484886, 01332 388 112
greig.wright@derbyshireccc.com

**County Age Group Squads
(9yrs to 17yrs) Co-ordinator
also responsible for District Development:**
Chris Porter, 01332 388 131
chris.porter@derbyshireccc.com

Academy Director:
Karl Krikken
karl.krikken@derbyshireccc.com

Performance Manager:
Chris Porter, 01332 388 131
chris.porter@derbyshireccc.com

Club Cricket Development Manager:
Mick Glenn 01332 388130 / 07976 504276
mick.glenn@derbyshireccc.com

**For all details on the Derbyshire Cricket Board
visit the Website on**
www.derbyshirecb.play-cricket.com

Coaching Centres:
The Gateway Centre, The County Ground,
Grandstand Road, Derby, DE21 6AF

Disabilities:
For any information on Disability Cricket in
Derbyshire please contact
Chairman:
Paul Roe, 01332 344 741 / 07908 046 772
14 Bretton Avenue, Littleover, Derby, DE23 6ED
Alternative Contact
Secretary:
Geoff Lane, 01332 764 929

Over 50's
Richard Owen, 01332 558 016

Durham County Cricket Club

County Ground

Address: County Ground, Riverside, Chester le Street, County Durham DH3 3QR

E mail reception@durhamccc.co.uk

Main telephone number 0191 387 1717

Web site address www.durhamccc.co.uk

Ticket Sales / Box Office:
0844 499 4466
box.office@durhamccc.co.uk

Match Day Catering:
0191 387 2839

Meetings and Events:
0191 387 2815

Hospitality / Corporate Bookings:
0191 387 2839

Shop:
0191 387 2877

Online Shop:
www.durhamccc.co.uk

Tours:
0844 499 4466

Press Enquiries:
0191 387 2873
yvette.thompson@durhamccc.co.uk

Officials:

Chief Executive:
David Harker, 0191 387 1717

Chairman:
Clive W. Leach C.B.E.

First Team Coach:
Geoff Cook

Captain:
Dale Benkenstein

Groundsman:
Dave Measor

Membership Department:
0844 499 4466

Box Office:
0844 499 4466

Travel Information:
Leave the A1(M) at junction 63 and follow the brown tourist information signs for the 'Riverside'.

Durham County Cricket Club

County Cricket

County Youth Department (Cricket Board)
0191 387 2868

Chief Cricket Board Administrator:
Hilary Nesbit 0191 387 2868

Women's Cricket Co-ordinator:
Pauline Peel 0191 387 2832

Cricket Development Manager (9yrs to 15yrs) :
Graeme Weeks 0191 387 2868

County Youth Squad Co-ordinator:
Bryan Arkle 0191 387 2868

Academy Coach:
John Windows

Cricket Administrator:
Ellen Johnson

Information on cricket for:

Disabilities:
Disabled spectators are able to bring a carer with them free of charge.

Community Coach (Disability Cricket)
Ron Young 0191 387 2868

Visually Impaired:
We offer complimentary commentary for the visually impaired at all home LV County Championship and Friends Provident Trophy matches. Places need to be booked in advance with the Visually Impaired Commentary Co-ordinator, Bernard Newman, on 01642 881 976

Hearing Loop:
A hearing loop is installed in the Members Facilities.

Outstanding achievements over the past 10 years:

2003 – The Riverside hosted its first Test Match, England v Zimbabwe.

2007 – Durham Dynamos claimed an historic victory against Hampshire Hawks at Lord's in the Friends Provident Trophy final, winning their first piece of silverware

Essex County Cricket Club

County Ground

Address: The Ford County Ground, New Writtle Street, Chelmsford, Essex, CM2 0PG

E-mail: administration.essex@ecb.co.uk

Main telephone number: 01245 252 420

Website address: www.essexcricket.org.uk

Ticket Sales:
01245 254 010

Matchday Catering:
01245 491 114

Meetings and Events:
01245 254 036

Hospitality / Corporate Bookings:
01245 254 001

Shop:
01245 254 020

Online Shop:
www.essexcricket.org.uk

Museum / Tours:
administration.essex@ecb.co.uk
for more on the Peter Edwards Museum and Library

Minor County Grounds:
Garon Park, Southend, Castle Park, Colchester

Officials:

President:
Doug Insole

Chairman:
Nigel Hilliard

Chief Executive:
David East

Director of Cricket Operations:
Alan Lilley

First Team Coach:
Paul Grayson

Batting Coach:
Graham Gooch

Captain:
Mark Pettini)

Head Groundsman:
Stuart Kerrison

Membership and Ticket Office Manager:
Eliza Rowley, 01245 254 010

Membership and Ticket Office Assistant:
Eleanor Farrow, 01245 254 010

Travel Information:
Go to
www.essexcricket.org.uk

Essex County Cricket Club

County Cricket

Cricket Operations:
01245 254 018

Director of Cricket Operations:
Alan Lilley

Cricket Board Secretary:
Graham Jelley

Chief Cricket Board Administrator:
Liz Wirth

Women's Cricket Co-ordinator:
Dave Letch

Academy Director:
John Childs

Coaching Centres:
Ashwell Graham Gooch Cricket Centre,
The Ford County Ground, New Writtle Street,
Chelmsford, CM2 0PG, 01245 254 028,
cricket.centre.essex@ecb.co.uk,
www.essexcricket.org.uk

Information on cricket for:
Disabilities
Over 50's
Over 60's
Visit the Essex County Cricket Cricket Board website
at www.eccb.org.uk for information

Glamorgan County Cricket Club

County Ground

Address: Glamorgan Cricket, SWALEC Stadium, Cardiff, CF11 9XR

E mail: info@glamorgancricket.co.uk

Main telephone number: 0871 282 3401

Web site address: www.glamorgancricket.com

Ticket Sales:
0871 282 3400

Meetings and Events:
0292 041 9315 / 9320

Hospitality / Corporate Bookings:
Hannah Morgan

Shop:
02920 226762

Online Shop:
www.mgmsports.co.uk

Officials:

Chief Executive:
Mike Fatkin
mike@glamorgancricket.co.uk

Chairman:
R Paul Russell

Captain:
David Hemp

Groundsman:
Len Smith

Travel Information:
go to
www.glamorgancricket.com
Contact Us link

Glamorgan County Cricket Club

County Cricket

Cricket Board of Wales:

County Youth Development:
Geoff Holmes, 029 2041 9336 / 07768 552 610
geoff@glamorgancricket.co.uk

Director of The Cricket Board of Wales Ltd:
Geoff Holmes, 029 2041 9336 / 07768 552 610
geoff@glamorgancricket.co.uk

Cricket Board Administrator:
Despina Asprou, 02920 419 341

Women and Girls Cricket Co-ordinator:
Sarah Ginn, 07977 674 832

County Age Group Squads
(9yrs to 17yrs) co-ordinator
also responsible for District Development:
Geoff Holmes, 029 2041 9336 / 07768 552 610
geoff@glamorgancricket.co.uk

Academy Director:
Richard Almond, 02920 419 340
richard@glamorgancricket.co.uk

Performance Manager:
Steve Watkin, 07854 704 876

Cricket Administrator:
Sarah Bell

Coaching Centres:
National Cricket Centre, Sophia Gardens,
Cardiff, CF11 9XR
0871 282 3401
info@glamorgancricket.co.uk
Web site address: www.glamorgancricket.com

Disabilities:
Paul Cartwright, 0777 3167 228

Over 50's
Ron Walton, 01685 386 094

Outstanding achievements over the past 10 years:

County Champions 1997

One Day League winners 2002 and 2004

Gloucestershire County Cricket Club

County Ground

Address: Nevil Road, Bristol BS7 9EJ

E mail: reception@glosccc.co.uk

Main telephone number: 0117 910 8000

Web site address: gloscricket.co.uk

Ticket Sales:
0117 910 8010
tickets@glosccc.co.uk

Sales & Marketing:
0117 910 8013
marketing@glosccc.co.uk

Conference Bookings:
0117 910 8025
conference@glosccc.co.uk

Meetings and Events:
0117 910 8025
conference@glosccc.co.uk

Hospitality / Corporate Bookings:
Kevin Ashley, 0117 910 8013

Shop:
0117 910 8020

Online Shop:
www.surridgesport.com/acatalog/Gloucestershire_
County_Cricket_Club.html

Officials:

Chief Executive:
T E M Richardson

Chairman:
John Light

Patron:
The Lord Vestey

Captain:
Jon Lewis

Vice Captain:
Alex Gidman

Groundsman:
Sean Williams

Membership Department:

Membership Secretary:
Vivienne Swann
0117 910 8017

Gloucestershire County Cricket Club

County Cricket

Cricket Board
Chairman
Trevor Crouch
0117 9732 626

Manager (performance):
Andy Stovold
0117 910 8004

Cricket development Manager:
Mike Bailey
01242 571 213
bails@gloscb.fsnet.co.uk

Youth County Squad (9yrs to 15yrs) co-ordinator also responsible for District Development:
Andy Stovold
0117 910 8004

Cricket Administration Manager:
Lizzie Allen
0117 910 8015

Hampshire County Cricket Club

County Ground

Address: The Rose Bowl, Botley Road, West End, Southampton, Hampshire, SO30 3XH

E mail: enquiries@rosebowlplc.com

Main telephone number: 023 8047 2002

Web site address: www.rosebowlplc.com

Ticket Sales:
tickets@rosebowlplc.com
0870 243 0291

Match Day Catering:
023 8047 1525

Meetings and Events:
023 8047 1525

Hospitality / Corporate Bookings:
023 8047 2009

Hampshire Shop:
023 8047 2002

Online Shop:
www.rosebowlplc.com

Officials:

Managing Director:
Glenn Delve, 023 8047 2002
glenn.delve@rosebowlplc.com

Chairman:
Rod Bransgrove

Secretary – Assistant to Chairman and Managing Director:
Collette Timson, 023 8047 0966
collette.timson@rosebowlplc.com

Director of Cricket:
Tim Tremlett, 023 8047 5614
tim.tremlett@rosebowlplc.com

First Team Coach:
Paul Terry, 023 8047 2002
paul.terry@rosebowlplc.com

Captain:
Dimitri Mascarenhas

Head Groundsman:
Nigel Gray, 023 8047 2002
nigel.gray@rosebowlplc.com

Benefit Year information:
John Crawley
www.johncrawley2008.co.uk

Travel information:
www.rosebowlplc.com

Hampshire County Cricket Club

HAMPSHIRE
CRICKET

County Cricket

Cricket Development Office (Cricket Board)

Cricket Development Manager:
Ben Thompson, 023 8047 5645
ben.thompson@rosebowlplc.com

Cricket Board Director:
Jeff Levick
jeff.levick@which.net

Chief Cricket Board Administrator:
Colin Savage, 023 8047 5816
colin.savage@rosebowlplc.com

Women and Girls Cricket Co-ordinator:
Mike Pollard, 023 8047 5632
michael.pollard@rosebowlplc.com

**Youth County Squad (9yrs to 15yrs) Co-ordinator
also responsible for District Development:**
Raj Maru
raj.maru@rosebowlplc.com
02380 475 630

Academy Director
Tony Middleton
tony.middleton@rosebowlplc.com

Performance Development Officer:
Raj Maru
raj.maru@rosebowlplc.com
02380 475 630

Coaching Centres:
Indoor School at The Rose Bowl
Andrew Milnes
andrew.milnes@rosebowlplc.com

Information on cricket for:

Disabilities, Over 50's, Over 60's
Greig Stewart, 0238 0475 653
greig.stewart@rosebowlplc.com

Kent County Cricket Club

County Ground

Address: St Lawrence Ground, Old Dover Road, Canterbury, Kent CT1 3NZ

E mail: kent@ecb.co.uk

Main telephone number: 01227 456886

Web site address: www.kentccc.com

Ticket Sales:
01227 456886

Match Day Catering:
01227 473612

Meetings and Events:
01227 473612

Hospitality / Corporate Bookings:
01227 456886

Shop:
01227 456886

Online Shop:
www.kentccc.com

Museum / Tours:
01227 456886 (via David Robertson, Hon. Curator)
Other = 01227 456886

Minor County Grounds:

Kent County Cricket Club Ground
Worsley Bridge Road
Beckenham BR3 1RL
Tel: 020 8650 8444

The Nevill Ground
Nevill Gate
Warwick Road
Tunbridge Wells TN2 5ES
01892 530 833 (Match Days Only)

Officials:

Chief Executive:
Paul Millman, 01227 456886
paul.millman.kent@ecb.co.uk

Chairman:
George M. Kennedy C.B.E.

Personal Assistant to Chief Executive:
Carolyn Dunne, 01227 456886
carolyn.dunne.kent@ecb.co.uk

Director of Cricket:
Graham Ford

Professional Cricket Manager:
Simon Willis

Captain:
Robert Key

Vice Captain:
Martin van Jaarsveld

Groundsman:
Mike Grantham

Membership Department:

Membership Secretary:
Mrs Jackie Symes - via main office

Travel Information:
Please refer to website: www.kentccc.com

Kent County Cricket Club

County Cricket

County Youth Department (Cricket Board):
01227 473618

Director of Cricket Development:
Jamie Clifford, 01227 473618
jamie.clifford.kent@ecb.co.uk

Cricket Board Administrator:
Stuart Mears: 01227 473618
stuart.mears.kent@ecb.co.uk

Women's Cricket Co-ordinator:
refer to Kent Cricket Board

Youth County Squad (9yrs to 15yrs) Co-ordinator also responsible for District Development:
Jason Weaver, 01227 473618
jason.weaver.kent@ecb.co.uk

Academy Director:
Phil Relf, 01227 473618
philip.relf.kent@ecb.co.uk

Cricket Administrator:
Roz Franklin, 01227 456886
ross.franklin.kent@ecb.co.uk

Coaching Centres, address, contact number and email (refer to Kent Cricket Board)

Schemes supporting cricket:
refer to Kent Cricket Board

Information on cricket for:
Disabilities
Over 50's
Over 60's
refer to Kent Cricket Board

Lancashire County Cricket Club

Lancashire County
Cricket Club

County Ground

Address: Old Trafford Cricket Ground, Talbot Road, Manchester M16 0PX

E mail: enquiries@lccc.co.uk

Main telephone number: 0161 282 4000

Web site address: www.lccc.co.uk

Ticket Sales:
0161 282 4040 or 08444 999 666

Match Day Catering:
0161 282 4020

Meetings and Events:
0161 282 4020

Hospitality / Corporate bBookings:
0161 282 4061

Shop:
0161 282 4050

Online Shop:
www.lcccshop.exitosports.com

Officials:

Director of Lancashire Cricket Board:
Andrew Hayhurst, 0161 282 4127
ahayhurst@lccc.co.uk

Secretary of Lancashire Cricket Board:
Neil Girvin , 0161 282 4029
ngirvin@lccc.co.uk

Travel Information:
Please refer to website:
www.lccc.co.uk

Lancashire County Cricket Club

Lancashire County Cricket Club

County Cricket

**Cricket Development Manager
for Greater Manchester**
Bobby Denning, 07764 922 804
bdenning@lccc.co.uk
(Lead Role: Disabilities Cricket)

**Cricket Development Manager
for Merseyside & West Lancashire:**
Paul Bryson, 07764 922 839
pbryson@lccc.co.uk
(Lead Role: Women and Girls Cricket)

**Cricket Development Manager
for NW and NE Lancashire**
Rudra Singh, 07764 922 841
rsingh@lccc.co.uk
(Lead Role: Kuick Cricket and Ethnic Minorities
Cricket)

Greater Manchester Cricket Support Officer:
David Hardman 0161 223 1002 / 07515 753 724
daveh@greatersport.co.uk

**Coach Education Co-ordinator and
Administrator:**
Tony Potter 0161 282 4021/ 07515 753 904
tpotter@lccc.co.uk

Business Manager:
Dipesh Asher 0161 282 4188 / 07894 585 009
dasher@lccc.co.uk

Leicestershire County Cricket Club

LEICESTERSHIRE
COUNTY CRICKET CLUB

County Ground

Address: County Ground, Grace Road, Leicester, LE2 8AD

E mail: enquiries@leicestershireccc.co.uk

Main telephone number: 0871 282 1879

Web site address: www.leicestershireccc.co.uk

Ticket Sales:
0871 282 1879

Match Day Catering:
0116 245 2439

Meetings and Events:
0116 245 2481

Hospitality / Corporate Bookings:
0116 245 2464

Shop:
0116 245 2453

Online Shop:
www.leicestershireccc.co.uk

Museum / Tours:
0116 283 1727

Minor County Grounds:
Oakham School, Hinckley Town

Officials:

Chief Executive:
Davis Smith
davidsmith@leicestershireccc.co.uk
Chairman:
Neil Davidson
rcn@mac.com
Operations Manager:
Phil Atkinson
philatkinson@leicestershireccc.co.uk
Senior Coach:
Tim Boon 0116 245 2465
timboon@leicestershireccc.co.uk
Head Coach / Academy Director:
Phil Whitticase: 0116 245 2444
philwhitticase@leicestershireccc.co.uk
Captain:
Paul Nixon
Vice Captain:
James Allenby

Groundsman:
Andy Whiteman

Membership Department:
Sussi Maguire

Travel Information:
From the M1 Motorway
M69/M1 Junction 21, take the A5460 along Narborough Road for approximately one mile. At the traffic lights at the junction of the Premier Travel Inn, turn right into Braunstone Lane. After approximately one mile, at the T-junction with Aylestone Road, turn left.

Finding Your Way Around
For entry via Curzon Road, follow the directions to Aylestone Road as above, but after 3/4 of a mile turn right on to Duncan Road followed by first left onto Curzon Road. The ground entrance is directly in front of you.

From the City Centre and the Railway Station
Take the A594 (Waterloo Way/Welford Road) heading south. Pass Leicester Tigers Rugby Club on your right and follow signs for A426 towards Rugby. Join Aylestone Road and pass car dealership on the left. After one mile, turn left into Duncan Road, followed by first left into Curzon Road. The ground entrance is directly in front of you.

Please note that there is no access to the ground from Grace Road itself and the Park Hill Drive entrance is closed except for match days.

Leicestershire County Cricket Club

County Cricket

Chief Cricket Board Administrator:
David Bailey 0116 244 2198

Women's Cricket Co-ordinator:
Neeta Patel 0116 244 2198

Youth County Squad (9yrs to 15yrs) co-ordinator also responsible for District Development:
Neeta Patel 0116 244 2198

Academy Director:
Phil Whitticase 0116 245 2444

Performance Manager:
Russell Cobb 07768 552580

Cricket Administrator:
Elaine Pickering 0116 245 2440

Coaching Centres:
0116 244 2198
neeta.patel@ecb.co.uk

Outstanding achievements over the past 10 years:

Leicestershire CCC
County Champions 1998
Twenty20 Cup winners 2004
Twenty20 Cup winners 2006

Middlesex County Cricket Club

County Ground

Address: Lord's Cricket Ground, London, NW8 8QN

E mail: enquiries@middlesexccc.com

Main telephone number: 020 7289 1300

Web site address: www.middlesexccc.com

Ticket Sales for Lord's:
020 7432 1000

Match Day Catering at Lord's:
020 7616 8500

Meetings and Events at Lord's:
020 7616 8500

Hospitality / Corporate Bookings at Lord's:
020 7616 8500
For outgrounds:
Lorraine Poole 020 7289 1300

Shop:
020 7289 1300

Online Shop:
www.middlesexccc.com

Museum:
020 7616 8658

Tours:
020 7616 8500

Minor County Grounds:
The Walker Ground, Southgate
Uxbridge Cricket Club, Uxbridge
Old Deer Park, Richmond
Ealing Cricket Club, Ealing
Merchant Taylor's School, Northwood
Radlett Cricket Club, Radlett
Shenley Cricket Club, Shenley
RAF Vine Lane, Uxbridge

Officials:

Secretary / Chief Executive:
Vinny Codrington
vinny.codrington@middlesexccc.com

Chairman:
Ian Lovett

First Teaam Coach:
Toby Radford

Captain:
Ed Smith

Vice Captain:
Ed Joyce

Groundsman:
Mick Hunt

Membership Department:
Membership line: 020 7286 5453

Travel Information:
Please refer to website: www.middlesexccc.com

Middlesex County Cricket Club

County Cricket

County Youth Department (Cricket Board):
020 7266 1650

Chief Cricket Board Administrator:
David Holland

Women's Cricket Co-ordinator:
Katie Berry

Youth County Squad (9yrs to 15yrs) Co-ordinator also responsible for District Development:
Phil Knappett

Academy Director:
Graeme West

Coaching Centres:
Middlesex Academy, Middlesex County Cricket Club, East End Road, Finchley, N3 2TA.
020 8346 8020.

Northamptonshire County Cricket Club

County Ground

Address: Abington Avenue, Northampton, NN1 4PR

E mail: reception@nccc.co.uk

Main telephone number: 01604 514455 or 01604 514444

Web site address: www.northantscricket.com

Ticket Sales:
01604 514455 or 514444
reception@nccc.co.uk

Match Day Catering:
Creations Events Caterers
01604 609294
creations.catering@virgin.net

Conference and Events:
01604 514490 / 609289
jacqueline.cabey@nccc.co.uk

Hospitality / Corporate Bookings:
01604 514481
graham.alsop@nccc.co.uk

Shop:
01604 609299
jenny.alsop@nccc.co.uk

Online Shop:
www.northantscricket.com

Minor County Grounds:
Campbell Park, Milton Keynes

Officials:

Chief Executive
Mark Tagg 01604 609266
mark.tagg@nccc.co.uk
PA - Dawn Conaty 01604 609266
dawn.conaty@nccc.co.uk

Chairman:
Martin Lawence

Director of Cricket & First Team Coach:
David Capel
david.capel@nccc.co.uk

Captain:
Nicky Boje

Groundsman:
Paul Marshall

Membership Department:
01604 514455 / 514444
reception@nccc.co.uk

Travel Information:
Northants Cricket is located two miles from the town centre and fifteen minutes from junction 15 of the M1. The train Station is located in the Town Centre and is on the main Birmingham to London line.

Northamptonshire County Cricket Club

County Cricket

County Youth Department (Cricket Board):

Cricket Board Director:
Ian Lucas – 01604 609256
ian.lucas@nccc.co.uk

Chief Cricket Board Administrator:
Tamsin Audouy 01604 609253
tamsin.audouy@nccc.co.uk

Youth County Squad (9yrs to 15yrs) Co-ordinator also responsible for District Development:
Ian Lucas 01604 609256
ian.lucas@nccc.co.uk

Academy Director
David Ripley
david.ripley@nccc.co.uk

Cricket Office:
Dawn Conaty – 01604 609266
dawn.conaty@nccc.co.uk

Coaching Centres:
Lynn Wilson Cricket Centre
The County Ground, Abington Avenue
Northampton, NN1 PR

Outstanding achievements over the past 10 years:

Double promotion in 2000
Runners up in NatWest Pro40 in 2006
Reached the Quarter Finals in the Twenty20 Cup for three consecutive years

The club have had a number of England age group represntives including
Mark Nelson,
Graeme White (England U19) and
Alex Wakely (England U17)

Monty Panesar has been picked for England

Nottinghamshire County Cricket Club

County Ground

Address: Nottinghamshire County Cricket Club, Trent Bridge, Nottingham, NG2 6AG

E mail: enquiries@nottsccc.co.uk

Main telephone number: 0115 982 3000

Web site address: www.nottsccc.co.uk or www.trentbridge.co.uk

Ticket Sales:
0870 168 8888
administration@nottsccc.co.uk

Meetings and Events:
0115 982 3042

Hospitality / Corporate Bookings:
0115 982 3002

Shop:
0115 981 9939

Museum / Tours:
0115 981 9939

Officials:

Chief Executive:
Derek Brewer 0115 982 3003

Deputy Chief Executive:
Lisa Pursehouse 0115 982 3048

Director of Cricket:
Mick Newell 0115 982 3005

Groundsman:
Steve Birks 0115 982 3000

Membership Department:
Bev Soar
Membership Services Co-ordinator 0870 168 8888

Travel Information:
There are frequent bus routes linking to the ground, with the rail station only a 20-minute walk away. East Midlands Airport is a 30-minute drive. Further transport information can be found at www.thebigwheel.org

Nottinghamshire County Cricket Club

County Cricket

County Youth Department (Cricket Board):
Call the Development Office on 0115 982 3046

Cricket Board Secretary:
Ron Lafbery

Club Development Officer:
Keith Tongue 0115 982 3000

Women's Cricket Co-ordinator:
Jane Islip

Youth County Squad (9yrs to 15yrs) Co-ordinator also responsible for District Development:
Stewart Burrows 0115 982 3000

Performance Manager:
Stewart Burrows 0115 982 3000

County Academy Director:
Chris Tolley 0115 982 3005

Coaching Centres:
Radcliffe Road Centre, Trent Bridge , Nottingham NG2 6AG
0115 982 3000
eddie.burke@nottsccc.co.uk (junior coaching)
stewart.burrows@nottsccc.co.uk (Coach Education)

Cricket in the Community:
Free visits by coaches to over 160 primary schools around the county.
Contact Eddie Burke for details

Cricket in the Classroom :
Free visits for Year 6 pupils to come and spend a day learning at Trent Bridge, using Howzat resources. Children learn Maths and English through a number of cricket-related activities, as well as receiving a guided tour of the ground and a games session at the end of the day.

School Visit Days:
Free offer for all schools to attend a day's play of an LV County Championship game and play on the field during the lunch interval.

Holiday and Weekly Coaching:
Regular sessions are held during most school holidays and also throughout the winter on weeknights and Saturday mornings.

Disabilities:
Eddie Burke 0115 982 3046

Over 50's
Joe Goodman

Outstanding achievements over the past 10 years:

Hosting the first ever Twenty20 Cup finals day in 2003 at Trent Bridge

Winning Division two of the Frizzell County Championship in 2004

Winning Division one of the Frizzell County Championship in 2005

Somerset County Cricket Club

County Ground

Address: The County Ground, Taunton, Somerset. TA1 1JT

E mail: info@somersetcountycc.co.uk

Main telephone number: 0845 337 1875

Web site address: www.somersetcountycc.co.uk

Ticket Sales:
0845 337 1875

Match Day Catering:
0845 337 1875

Meetings and Events:
0845 337 1875

Hospitality / Corporate Bookings:
0845 337 1875

Shop:
01823 337 597

Online Shop:
www.somerset-countysports.com

Museum / Tours:
01823 275 893

Minor County Grounds:
Taunton Vale CC, North Perrot CC

Officials:

President:
R. C. Kerslake

Chief Executive:
Richard Gould

Chairman:
A. J. Nash

Director of Cricket:
Brian Rose

Head Coach:
Andy Hurry

Captain:
Justin Langer

Groundsman:
Phil Frost

Membership Department:
0845 337 1875

Travel Information:
10 minutes walk from Taunton station
10 minutes from junction 25 M5

Somerset County Cricket Club

Somerset
COUNTY CRICKET CLUB

County Cricket

Somerset Cricket Board:
01823 352 266

County Youth Department (Cricket Board):
Andrew Moulding

Cricket Board Vice Chairman:
Andrew Curtis

Chief Cricket Board Administrator:
Andrew Moulding

Women's Cricket Co-ordinator:
Lisa Pagett 0784 844 746

Youth County Squad (9yrs to 15yrs) Co-ordinator also responsible for District Development:
Peter Sanderson

Academy Director:
Jason Kerr

Performance Manager:
Peter Sanderson

Cricket Administrator:
Andrew Moulding

Coaching Centres:
Centre of Cricketing Excellence
The County Ground, Taunton, Somerset, TA1 1JT
01823 352 266

Information on cricket for

Disabilities:
Julian Bellew

Over 50's
Roger Snelling

Over 60's
Roger Snelling

Outstanding achievements over the past 10 years:

C&G Trophy Runners Up 2000

C&G Trophy Winners 2001

County Championship Runners Up 2001

C&C Trophy Runners Up 2002

Twenty20 Cup Winners 2005

County Championship Division 2 Winners 2007

NatWest Pro40 - Promoted to Division 1 2007

Surrey County Cricket Club

County Ground

Address: The Brit Insurance Oval, Kennington, London, SE11 5SS

E mail: enquiries@surreycricket.com

Main telephone number: 08712 461 100

Web site address: www.surreycricket.com

General Enquiries:
08712 461 100
enquiries@surreycricket.com

Ticket Hotline:
08712 461 100 option 1
tickets@surreycricket.com

Sponsorship:
08712 461 100
tlangenegger@surreycricket.com

Membership Office:
08712 461 100 option 2
membership@surreycricket.com

Oval Events, Conference and Events:
08712 461 100 option 4
enquiries@ovalevents.com

The Oval Shop:
08712 461 100 option 5
shop@surreycricket.com

Coaching Courses:
08712 461 100 option 6

Officials:

Chief Executive:
Paul Sheldon

Chairman:
David Stewart

FirstTeam Coach:
Alan Butcher

Captain:
Mark Butcher

Groundsman:
Bill Gordon

Travel Information:
The Brit Insurance Oval is easily accessible from the West End, the City and all South East Counties.
By Underground – Take the Northern Line from the City or Central London to the Oval tube station. The main entrance to the ground is 100 metres on your left. The ground is also a ten minute walk from Vauxhall tube, on the Victoria line.
By Rail – Take South West Trains to Vauxhall station, which is well served by trains throughout Surrey and Hampshire as well as from greater London.
By Bus – Route number 36 and 185 stop outside the ground and other local services stop nearby.
By Bike – Limited bike parking is available for spectator use at the Brit Oval.
By Car – The ground is on the A202, near the junction with the A3 and A24, south of Vauxhall Bridge and ten minutes from Victoria and Waterloo. No match day car parking is available at or near the ground and we advise all customers to use public transport.
By Coach – Details of coach parking and dropping off facilities are available on request

Surrey County Cricket Club

County Cricket

County Youth Department (Cricket Board):
08712 461 100

Cricket Board Chair:
Tony Pannell, 01328 820 227
t.pannell@dsl.pipex.com

Performance Administrator:
Dave Sheppard, 020 7820 5734
dsheppard@surreycricket.com

Women's Cricket Co-ordinator:
Sharon Eyers, 07768 558 045
seyers@surreycricket.com

Director of Development:
Paul Taylor, 020 7820 5683
ptaylor@surreycricket.com

Development Administrator:
Sarah Midwinter, 020 7820 5684
smidwinter@surreycricket.com

Academy Director:
Gareth Townsend, 020 7820 5762
gtownsend@surreycricket.com

Performance Officer:
David Court
dcourt@surreycricket.com

Coaching Centres:
Ken Barrington Cricket Centre
The Brit Insurance Oval
Kennington
London
SE11 5SS
08712 461100
kbccadministrator@surreycricket.com

Surrey County Cricket Centre:
George Abbot School
Woodruff Avenue
Guildford
Surrey
GU1 1XX
01483 598880
guildford@surreycricket.com

Information on cricket for:

Disabilities:
Sharon Eyers, 07768 558045
seyers@surreycricket.com

Over 50's / 60's
Brian Aspital, 01372 454859
brian@aspitaL.fslife.co.uk

Sussex County Cricket Club

County Ground

Address: The County Ground, Eaton Road, Hove, East Sussex BN3 3AN

E mail info@sussexcricket.co.uk

Main telephone number 0844 264 0202

Web site address www.sussexcricket.co.uk

Ticket Sales:
0844 264 0206

Match Day Catering:
0844 264 1736

Meetings and Events:
0844 264 1736

Hospitality / Corporate Bookings:
0844 264 0201

Shop:
0844 264 1734

Online Shop:
www.sussexcricket.co.uk

Museum / Tours / Library / Museum:
01273 827 112

Minor County Grounds:
Horsham Cricket Club
Arundel Castle Cricket Club
Hastings, Horntye Park

Officials:

Chief Executive:
Gus Mackay
gus.mackay@sussexcricket.co.uk

Chairman:
David Green

Secretary PA to Chief Exec
Sarah McKee 01273 827 130

Pro Cricket Manager:
Mark Robinson

Club Coach:
Mark Davis

Captain:
Chris Adams

Vice Captain:
Michael Yardy

Groundsman:
Lawrence Gosling

Membership Department:
Patricia Carr 0871 282 2003

Travel Information:
0844 264 0206

Sussex County Cricket Club

County Cricket

County Youth Department (Cricket Board):
katie.sykes@sussexcricket.co.uk
01273 827 113

Cricket Board Development Manager:
Andy Hobbs
andy.hobbs@sussexcricket.co.uk

Cricket Development Officer:
John Stock 01273 827 115
john.stock@sussexcricket.co.uk
Tim Shutt 01273 827 117
tim.shutt@sussexcricket.co.uk

Women's Cricket Co-ordinator:
Charlotte Burton 07974 420 224

**Youth County Squad (9yrs to 15yrs) Co-ordinator
also responsible for District Development:**
Siobhan Edgar
siobhan.edgar@sussexcricket.co.uk

Academy Director:
Keith Greenfield
keith.Greenfield@sussexcricket.co.uk

Performance Manager:
Keith Greenfield
keith.greenfield@sussexcricket.co.uk

Cricket Development Administrator:
Katie Sykes 01273 827 113
katie.sykes@sussexcricket.co.uk

Coaching Centres:
Colin Bowley, Indoor School Manager,
Indoor School, Sussex CCC, Eaton Road,
Hove, East Sussex BN3 3AN

Schemes supporting cricket:
RDF Roadshow
MGM Coaching schemes
Community Coaching schemes
U10s – Cricket Telecom
Schools – Chance to Shine
Competitions - Asda Kwik Cricket
For more information contact
katie.sykes@sussexcricket.co.uk
01273 827 113

Information on cricket for:

**Disabilities – Visually impaired –
Sussex Sharks junior / senior teams:**
Andy Dalby-Welsh
07786 238168
andy@dalby-welsh.fsnet.co.uk

Bexhill visually impaired juniors:
john.stock@sussexcricket.co.uk

Over 50s & Over 60s
both teams play in County Championships.
Contact for both is
Barry Peay 01403 790444
peay@waitrose.com

Warwickshire County Cricket Club

County Ground

Address: The County Ground, Edgbaston, Birmingham, B5 7QU

E mail info@edgbaston.com

Main telephone number 0870 062 1902

Web site address www.edgbaston.com

Ticket Sales:
0870 062 1902
tickets@edgbaston.com

Match Day Catering:
0870 062 1902

Meetings and Events:
0870 062 1902
events@edgbaston.com

Hospitality / Corporate Bookings:
0870 062 1902
hospitality@edgbaston.com

Shop:
0870 062 1902

Online Shop:
www.thecricketshop.co.uk

Museum / Tours:
museum@edgbaston.com

Officials:

Chief Executive:
Colin Povey

Chairman:
Neil Houghton

Director of Cricket:
Ashley Giles

Captain:
Darren Maddy

Groundsman:
Steve Rouse

Membership Department:
membership@edgbaston.com

Travel Information:
www.thebears.com

Warwickshire County Cricket Club

County Cricket

County Youth Department (Cricket Board):
0121 446 3615

Cricket Board Director:
Richard Cox

Chief Cricket Board Administrator:
Angela Sweeney

Women's Cricket Co-ordinator:
Kelly Evenson

Youth County Squad (9yrs to 15yrs) Co-ordinator also responsible for District Development:
Richard Cox

Academy Director:
Richard Cox

Coaching Centres:
Address, contact number and email same as above at County Ground

Information on cricket for:

Disabilities:
Andy Wyles : 0121 446 3615

Over 50's
Alan Oakman
alanoakman@edgbaston.com

Outstanding achievements over the past 10 years:

County Champions 2004

First Class Counties 2nd XI Trophy 2006

Worcestershire County Cricket Club

County Ground

Address: New Road, Worcester, WR2 4QQ

E mail: admin@wccc.co.uk

Main telephone number: 01905 748 474

Web site address: www.wccc.co.uk

Ticket Sales:
01905 337 921
jo-ann.harris@wccc.co.uk

Match Day Catering:
01905 337 940
catering@wccc.co.uk

Meetings and Events:
01905 337 940
catering@wccc.co.uk

Hospitality / Corporate Bookings:
01905 337 933
jodi.brandwood@wccc.co.uk

Shop:
01905 337 922
jo-ann.harris@wccc.co.uk

Online Shop:
www.newroad1.co.uk

Minor County Grounds:
Barnt Green CC, 0121 445 1684
Bromsgrove CC, 01527 878 252
Kidderminster CC, 01562 824 175
Old Hill CC, 01384 566 827
Ombersley CC

Officials:

Chairman:
Martyn Price

Chief Executive:
Mark Newton
mark.newton@wccc.co.uk

PA to Chief Executive:
Joan Grundy
joan.grundy@wccc.co.uk

Director of Cricket:
Steve Rhodes

Assistant Coach / Academy Director:
Damian D'Oliveira

Captain:
Vikram Solanki

Vice Captain:
Gareth Batty

Head Groundsman:
Tim Packwood

Membership Department:
Jo-Ann Harris

Membership Services Manager:
Worcestershire CCC, New Road, Worcester, WR2 4QQ
01905 337 922
jo-ann.harris@wccc.co.uk

Travel Information:
Exit M5 at Junction 7 towards Worcester. Follow the 'broken stumps' signposts.

Worcestershire County Cricket Club

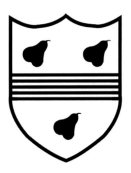

County Cricket

Worcestershire Cricket Board (WCB):
Stuart Lampitt
01905 337 923
stuart.lampitt@wccc.co.uk

Cricket Board Administrator:
Chris Marsh

Cricket Development Officer:
Stuart Lampitt

Worcestershire Young Cricketers Chairman:
Richard Wood

Worcestershire Cricket Centre:
Prince Henry's High School
Victoria Avenue, Evesham, Worcs WR11 4QH
01386 45074
sports@princehenrys.worcs.sch.uk

Information on cricket for:

Disabilities and Over 50's
go to WCB website or phone office

Outstanding achievements over the past 10 years:

Double promotion to first division of both league
competitions in 2006

NatWest Pro40 division one winners 2007

Yorkshire County Cricket Club

County Ground

Address: Headingley Carnegie Stadium, Leeds, LS6 3BU.

E mail: cricket@yorkshireccc.com

Main telephone number: 0870 429 6774

Web site address: www.yorkshireccc.com

Ticket Sales:
0871 222 0994

Shop:
0113 230 6334

Online Shop:
www.yorkshireccc.com/shop

Commercial Manager:
James Hogg
0113 203 3607

Officials:

Chief Executive:
Mr. S.M. Regan
stewart@yorkshireccc.com

Chairman:
Mr. C.J. Graves

Secretary:
Mr. B. Bouttell

Director of Cricket:
M. Moxon

First Team Coaches:
K. Sharp, S. Oldham

Captain:
D. Gough

Vice Captain:
A. McGrath

Groundsman:
A. Fogarty

Membership Department:
Lisa Jackson
0113 203 3631

Travel Information:
www.yorkshireccc.com/find_us

THE YORKSHIRE COUNTY CRICKET CLUB

County Cricket

County Youth Department (Cricket Board):
YCB - Bradford & Bingley Cricket Centre,
St. Michael's Lane,
Leeds, LS6 3BU
0113 203 3610

Chief Executive:
I. M. Chappell
07885 369 600
ichappell@ycb-yca.fsnet.co.uk

Administrator:
H. Clayton
07721 527 727

Women's Cricket Co-ordinator:
Will Kitchen
0113 203 3610

Development Director:
Andrew Watson
07966 173 525

Youth County Squad (9yrs to 15yrs) Co-ordinator also responsible for District Development:

Academy Director:
R. Wilkinson
0113 203 3628

Coaching Centres:
Bradford & Bingley
Indoor Cricket Centre, St. Michael's Lane,
Headingley, Leeds, LS6 3BU.
Andy Rowsell
0113 203 3609

Outstanding achievements over the past 10 years:

County Champions: 2001

Promoted to Div. 1: 2005

C & G Winners: 2002

M.C.C. - Lord's

Address: M.C.C. - Lord's Cricket Ground, London NW8 8QN

Main telephone number: 020 7616 8500

Web site address: www.lords.org

Ticket Sales:
020 7432 1000
ticketing@mcc.org.uk

Match Day Catering:
020 7616 8598

Hospitality / Corporate Bookings:
020 7616 8598
hospitality@mcc.org.uk

Meetings & Events:
020 7616 8501
events@lords.org

Lord's Shop:
020 7616 8570

Online Shop:
www.lords.org

Museum / Tours:
020 7616 8595
tours@mcc.org.uk

Sponsorship & Advertising:
020 7616 8561
marketing@mcc.org.uk

Officials:

Secretary & Chief Executive:
Keith Bradshaw

Chairman:
Charles Fry

Head of Cricket:
John Stephenson

Head Groundsman:
Mick Hunt

England and Wales Cricket Board

Address: England and Wales Cricket Board, Lords Cricket Ground, Saint Johns Wood, London, NW8 8QZ

Main telephone number: 020 7432 1200

Web site address: www.ecb.co.uk

Officials:

Chairman
Giles Clarke

Chief Executive
David Collier

**Managing Director England and
Deputy Chief Executive**
Hugh Morris

Managing Director Cricket Partnerships
Mike Gatting

Commercial Director
John Perera

Finance Director
Brian Havill

Head of Venue Contracts
Gordon Hollins

Head of Corporate Communication
Colin Gibson

Head of Womens Cricket
Clare Connor

Head of Information Technology
Chris Hoad

Tournament Director World T20 Championships
Steve Elworthy

Team England Director
Peter Moores

National Performance Centre, Loughborough,
University, Loughborough, Leicestershire, LE11 3TU
01509 228664

ECB Development Office
County Cricket Ground, Old Trafford, Manchester,
M16 0PX
0161 873 7682

ECB Coaches Association
County Cricket Ground, Edgbaston,
Birmingham, B5 7QX
0121 440 4332

National Disability Cricket Manager
Ian Martin
England and Wales Cricket Board
Lord's Cricket Ground London NW8 8QZ
ian.martin@ecb.co.uk
07824 600 325

Professional Cricketers' Association

Address: PCA, 5 Utopia Village, 7 Chalcot Road, Primrose Hill, London NW1 8LH

Web site address: www.thepca.co.uk

Commercial enquiries
Tom Greenwood
020 7449 4226

Player Services
Rachel Newnham
020 7449 4229

Cricket Issues
Jason Ratcliffe
07768 558 050

Events enquiries
Fiona Holdsworth
020 7449 4221
Fax: 020 7586 8520

Chairman (Cricket)
Dougie Brown
07785 527 100

Group Chairman
Tim O'Gorman
07715 170 030
togorman@thepca.co.uk

Chief Executive
Sean Morris
smorris@thepca.co.uk
07734 930 898 / 020 7449 4231

Assistant Chief Executive
Jason Ratcliffe
07768 558 050 / 020 7449 4228
jratcliffe@thepca.co.uk

Events Director
Steve Marsh
07787 152 998
smarsh@thepca.co.uk

Director
Gladstone Small
07808 910 606
gsmall@thepca.co.uk

Legal Director
Ian Smith
07798 698 201
ismith@thepca.co.uk

PCA Vice President - Health Trust
David Graveney OBE
07850 000 189
dgraveney@thepca.co.uk

Commercial Director
Johnny Grave
07768 558 038 / 020 7449 4224
jgrave@thepca.co.uk

Events Manager
Fiona Holdsworth
020 7449 4221
fholdsworth@thepca.co.uk

**Senior Executive PCA Masters &
New Business Director**
Paul Prichard
07779 026 562 / 020 7449 4234
pprichard@thepca.co.uk

Senior Executive & Deputy Editor, All Out Cricket
Jimmy Hindson
07866 241 241
jhindson@thepca.co.uk

Professional Cricketers' Association

Accounts
Elaine Nelson
01743 289 185
enelson@thepca.co.uk

Sponsorship Services Manager
Tom Greenwood
020 7449 4226
tgreenwood@thepca.co.uk

Player Services Executive
Rachel Newnham
07881 881 531 / 020 7449 4229
rnewnham@thepca.co.uk

Player Services Executive - Team England
Emma Barnes
020 7449 4230
ebarnes@thepca.co.uk

Sponsorship Services Executive
Natasha Elliott
020 7449 4227
nelliott@thepca.co.uk

Events Coordinator
Liz Wood
020 7449 4222
lwood@thepca.co.uk

Player Services Assistant
Lucy Cooke
020 7449 4235
lcooke@thepca.co.uk

Non-Executive Director
Richard Bevan
rbevan@thepca.co.uk

Non-Executive Director
Phil Jansen
Phillip.Jansen@Sodexho-uk.com

PCA Officers

Patron:
Rt Hon John Major CH

President: Ian Botham OBE

Chairman: Dougie Brown

Vice Chairman: TBC

Honourary Life Founder Member & Vice President: Fred Rumsey

Senior Vice President: Harold Goldblatt

Vice Presidents: David Graveney, Alec Stewart , Matthew Fleming, Lawrie Doffman, Tim Curtis, Geoff Cook, Peter Walker, Richard Bevan

The Cricketers' Association Charity
Chairman: David Graveney

Trustees: Geoff Cook, John Lever, Alan Oakman, Jim Parks, Peter Walker, Jim Watts, Harold Goldblatt

FORGET THE
IPL AUCTIONS

WHO REALLY ARE THE
MOST VALUABLE PLAYERS?

MORE PROSPECTS
MORE OPPORTUNITIES

The PCA MVP ranking system now encompasses both County MVP and England MVP - giving players hundreds of opportunities to increase their value and ranking throughout the domestic and international season.

The MVP's are based on a cumulative points system, rewarding all valued elements that are imperative to win cricket matches.

Runs, strike rates, wickets, economy rates and catches, all in one formula = MVP

To view the current results for both County MVP and England MVP or for more info simply visit:
www.thepca.co.uk

pca mvp
MOST VALUABLE PLAYER
ECB

ENGLAND mvp
MOST VALUABLE PLAYER

2009

Yearbook and Desk Diary

2009

	January	February	March	April	May	June
M						1
Tu						2
W				1		3
Th	1			2		4
F	2			3	1	5
Sa	3			4	2	6
Su	4	1	1	5	3	7
M	5	2	2	6	4	8
Tu	6	3	3	7	5	9
W	7	4	4	8	6	10
Th	8	5	5	9	7	11
F	9	6	6	10	8	12
Sa	10	7	7	11	9	13
Su	11	8	8	12	10	14
M	12	9	9	13	11	15
Tu	13	10	10	14	12	16
W	14	11	11	15	13	17
Th	15	12	12	16	14	18
F	16	13	13	17	15	19
Sa	17	14	14	18	16	20
Su	18	15	15	19	17	21
M	19	16	16	20	18	22
Tu	20	17	17	21	19	23
W	21	18	18	22	20	24
Th	22	19	19	23	21	25
F	23	20	20	24	22	26
S	24	21	21	25	23	27
S	25	22	22	26	24	28
M	26	23	23	27	25	29
Tu	27	24	24	28	26	30
W	28	25	25	29	27	
Th	29	26	26	30	28	
F	30	27	27		29	
Sa	31	28	28		30	
Su			29		31	
M			30			
Tu			31			

July	August	September	October	November	December	
						M
		1			1	Tu
1		2			2	W
2		3	1		3	Th
3		4	2		4	F
4	1	5	3		5	Sa
5	2	6	4	1	6	Su
6	3	7	5	2	7	M
7	4	8	6	3	8	Tu
8	5	9	7	4	9	W
9	6	10	8	5	10	Th
10	7	11	9	6	11	F
11	8	12	10	7	12	Sa
12	9	13	11	8	13	Su
13	10	14	12	9	14	M
14	11	15	13	10	15	Tu
15	12	16	14	11	16	W
16	13	17	15	12	17	Th
17	14	18	16	13	18	F
18	15	19	17	14	19	Sa
19	16	20	18	15	20	Su
20	17	21	19	16	21	M
21	18	22	20	17	22	Tu
22	19	23	21	18	23	W
23	20	24	22	19	24	Th
24	21	25	23	20	25	F
25	22	26	24	21	26	S
26	23	27	25	22	27	S
27	24	28	26	23	28	M
28	25	29	27	24	29	Tu
29	26	30	28	25	30	W
30	27		29	26	31	Th
31	28		30	27		F
	29		31	28		Sa
	30			29		Su
	31			30		M
						Tu

Monday

29

Tuesday

30

Wednesday

31

New Year's Eve

Thursday

1

New Year's Day

Friday

2

Bank Holiday Scotland

Saturday

3

Sunday

4

Sachin (detail), *oil on canvas*

	Monday
	5
	Tuesday
	6
	Wednesday
	7
	Thursday
	8
	Friday
	9

Saturday	Sunday
10	**11**

Freddie 24x36ins, *oil on canvas*

	Monday **12**
	Tuesday **13**
	Wednesday **14**
	Thursday **15**
	Friday **16**
Saturday **17**	Sunday **18**

Keeper 18x12ins, *oil on canvas*

Monday

19

Tuesday

20

Wednesday

21

Thursday

22

Friday

23

Saturday

24

Sunday

25

Slogger 12x12ins, *oil on canvas,* courtesy of Richard and Louise Wynne-Griffith

	Monday 26
	Tuesday 27
	Wednesday 28
	Thursday 29
	Friday 30
Saturday 31	Sunday 1

Urban 30x40ins, *oil on canvas*

	Monday **2**
	Tuesday **3**
	Wednesday **4**
	Thursday **5**
	Friday **6**
Saturday **7**	Sunday **8**

Celebration 24x36ins, *oil on canvas*

Monday

9

Tuesday

10

Wednesday

11

Thursday

12

Friday

13

Saturday

14

St. Valentine's Day

Sunday

15

Second Innings, *sketch*

Monday
16

Tuesday
17

Wednesday
18

Thursday
19

Friday
20

Saturday
21

Sunday
22

Boots 12x8ins, *oil on board*

	Monday
	23

	Tuesday
	24

	Wednesday
	25
	Ash Wednesday

	Thursday
	26

	Friday
	27

Saturday	Sunday
28	**1**
	St. David's Day

ODI South Africa v Zimbabwe 2003 The Rose Bowl 36x48ins, *oil on canvas*

Monday

2

Tuesday

3

Wednesday

4

Thursday

5

Friday

6

Saturday

7

Sunday

8

Great Expectations 12x6ins, *oil on board*, courtesy of David and Jean Pierce

Monday

9

Tuesday

10

Wednesday

11

Thursday

12

Friday

13

Saturday

14

Sunday

15

Scorers 10x12ins, *oil on board*

Monday
16

Tuesday
17
St. Patrick's Day

Wednesday
18

Thursday
19

Friday
20

Saturday
21

Sunday
22
Mothering Sunday

Lord's Taverners 36x24ins, *oil on canvas*

Monday

23

Tuesday

24

Wednesday

25

Thursday

26

Friday

27

Saturday

28

Sunday

29

British Summer Time - clocks go forward

Team Talk 18x24ins, *oil on board*

Monday

30

Tuesday

31

Wednesday

1

Thursday

2

Friday

3

Saturday

4

Sunday

5

Matthew Hoggard 36x24ins, *oil on canvas*

Monday

6

Tuesday

7

Wednesday

8

Thursday

9

Friday

IO

Good Friday

Saturday

II

Sunday

I2

Easter Sunday

Chigwell Essex 10x12ins, *oil on board*

Monday

13

Easter Monday

Tuesday

14

Wednesday

15

Thursday

16

Friday

17

Saturday

18

Sunday

19

Sachin Tendulkar 12x12ins, *oil on board*, courtesy of Lucy and Sanjay Beri

Monday

20

Tuesday

21

Wednesday

22

Thursday

23

St. George's Day

Friday

24

Saturday

25

Sunday

26

Umpire 12x12ins, *oil on canvas*, courtesy of Map Black

Monday

27

Tuesday

28

Wednesday

29

Thursday

30

Friday

I

Saturday

2

Sunday

3

Last Over 12x12ins, *oil on canvas*

Monday

4

May Day Holiday

Tuesday

5

Wednesday

6

Thursday

7

Friday

8

Saturday

9

Sunday

10

Cricket Ball 40x30ins, *oil on canvas*

	Monday **11**
	Tuesday **12**
	Wednesday **13**
	Thursday **14**
	Friday **15**
Saturday **16**	Sunday **17**

The Groundsman 10x15ins, *oil on board*

Monday
18

Tuesday
19

Wednesday
20

Thursday
21

Friday
22

Saturday
23

Sunday
24

Crawley and Carberry 17x18ins, *oil on board*

Monday

25

Spring Bank Holiday

Tuesday

26

Wednesday

27

Thursday

28

Friday

29

Saturday

30

Sunday

31

Frosty 12x16ins, *oil on board*

Monday

1

Tuesday

2

Wednesday

3

Thursday

4

Friday

5

Saturday

6

Sunday

7

Waiting to Bat 14x12ins, *oil on board*

Monday

8

Tuesday

9

Wednesday

10

Thursday

11

Friday

12

Saturday

13

Sunday

14

Scoreboard 30x40ins, *oil on canvas*

	Monday **15**
	Tuesday **16**
	Wednesday **17**
	Thursday **18**
	Friday **19**
Saturday **20**	Sunday **21** *Father's Day* *Longest Day*

Padding Up 18x18ins, *oil on canvas*

	Monday **22**
	Tuesday **23**
	Wednesday **24** *4 day game Australia v Sussex (Hove)*
	Thursday **25** *4 day game Australia v Sussex (Hove)*
	Friday **26** *4 day game Australia v Sussex (Hove)*

Saturday **27** *4 day game Australia v Sussex (Hove)*	Sunday **28**

King of Spain 20x24ins, *oil on canvas*

Monday

29

Tuesday

30

Wednesday

1

4 day game Australia v England Lions (Worcester)

Thursday

2

4 day game Australia v England Lions (Worcester)

Friday

3

4 day game Australia v England Lions (Worcester)

Saturday

4

4 day game Australia v England Lions (Worcester)

Sunday

5

Balls 6x8ins, *oil on paper,* courtesy of Penny and David Hughes

Monday

6

Tuesday

7

Wednesday

8

1st npower Test Match - Cardiff - England v Australia

Thursday

9

1st npower Test Match - Cardiff - England v Australia

Friday

10

1st npower Test Match - Cardiff - England v Australia

Saturday

11

1st npower Test Match - Cardiff - England v Australia

Sunday

12

1st npower Test Match - Cardiff - England v Australia

Huddle 20x24ins, *oil on canvas*, courtesy of Ashley Giles

Monday

13

Tuesday

14

Wednesday

15

Thursday

16

2nd npower Test Match - Lord's - England v Australia

Friday

17

2nd npower Test Match - Lord's - England v Australia

Saturday

18

2nd npower Test Match - Lord's - England v Australia

Sunday

19

2nd npower Test Match - Lord's - England v Australia

Friday Evening 18x24ins, *oil on canvas*

Monday

20

2nd npower Test Match - Lord's - England v Australia

Tuesday

21

Wednesday

22

Thursday

23

Friday

24

3 day game First Class Counties Select 11 v Australia (Northampton)

Saturday

25

*3 day game First Class Counties
Select 11 v Australia (Northampton)*

Sunday

26

*3 day game First Class Counties
Select 11 v Australia (Northampton)*

The Picnic 18x20ins, *oil on board*, courtesy of David and Jean Pierce

Monday

27

Tuesday

28

Wednesday

29

Thursday

30

3rd npower Test Match - Edgbaston - England v Australia

Friday

31

3rd npower Test Match - Edgbaston - England v Australia

Saturday

1

3rd npower Test Match - Edgbaston
England v Australia

Sunday

2

3rd npower Test Match - Edgbaston
England v Australia

Alastair Cook 12x14ins, *oil on board*

Monday

3

3rd npower Test Match - Edgbaston - England v Australia

Tuesday

4

Wednesday

5

Thursday

6

Friday

7

4th npower Test Match - Headingley - England v Australia

Saturday

8

4th npower Test Match - Headingley
England v Australia

Sunday

9

4th npower Test Match - Headingley
England v Australia

Brian Lara 10x12ins, *oil on board*

Monday

10

4th npower Test Match - Headingley - England v Australia

Tuesday

11

4th npower Test Match - Headingley - England v Australia

Wednesday

12

Thursday

13

Friday

14

Saturday

15

2 day game Kent v Australia (Canterbury)

Sunday

16

2 day game Kent v Australia (Canterbury)

A Welcome Pint 10x15ins, *oil on board*

Monday

17

Tuesday

18

Wednesday

19

Thursday

20

5th npower Test Match - Oval - England v Australia

Friday

21

5th npower Test Match - Oval - England v Australia

Saturday

22

5th npower Test Match - Oval - England v Australia

Sunday

23

5th npower Test Match - Oval - England v Australia

Before the Game 18x24ins, *oil on board*

Monday

24

5th npower Test Match - Oval - England v Australia

Tuesday

25

Wednesday

26

Thursday

27

Friday

28

ODI Scotland v Australia (Edinburgh)

Saturday

29

Sunday

30

1st NatWest International Twenty20 - Old Trafford

Sachin Tandulkar 8x10ins, *oil on board*, courtesy of James and Nikki Prichard

	Monday
	31
	Late Summer Holiday

	Tuesday
	1
	2nd NatWest International Twenty20 - Old Trafford - Floodlit

	Wednesday
	2

	Thursday
	3

	Friday
	4
	1st NatWest Series Day/Night - Brit Oval

Saturday	Sunday
5	**6**
	2nd NatWest Series - Lord's

Sunday Afternoon 16x12ins, *oil on board*

Monday

7

Tuesday

8

Wednesday

9

3rd NatWest Series Day/Night - Rose Bowl

Thursday

10

Friday

11

Saturday

12

4th NatWest Series - Lord's

Sunday

13

Boots 8x12ins, *oil on board*

Monday

14

Tuesday

15

5th NatWest Series Day/Night - Trent Bridge

Wednesday

16

Thursday

17

6th NatWest Series Day/Night - Trent Bridge

Friday

18

Saturday

19

Sunday

20

7th NatWest Series - Durham

The Rosebowl - County Ground Hampshire 36x48ins, *oil on canvas*, courtesy of John Crawley

Monday

2I

Australian Team Departs

Tuesday

22

Wednesday

23

Thursday

24

Friday

25

Saturday

26

Sunday

27

Sir Vivian Richards 40x30ins, *oil on board*

Monday **28**	
Tuesday **29**	
Wednesday **30**	
Thursday **1**	
Friday **2**	
Saturday **3**	Sunday **4**

The Good Old Days 16x12ins, *oil on canvas*, courtesy of Julian and Ann Dickinson

October

Monday
5

Tuesday
6

Wednesday
7

Thursday
8

Friday
9

Saturday
10

Sunday
11

Two to Win 24x36ins, *oil on canvas*, courtesy of Ashley Giles

	Monday **12**
	Tuesday **13**
	Wednesday **14**
	Thursday **15**
	Friday **16**
Saturday **17**	Sunday **18**

OCS Stand The Oval 12x30ins, *oil on canvas*

Monday

19

Tuesday

20

Wednesday

21

Thursday

22

Friday

23

Saturday

24

Sunday

25

British Summer Time ends - clocks go back

Young Cricketer 12x8ins, *oil on board*

Monday

26

Tuesday

27

Wednesday

28

Thursday

29

Friday

30

Saturday

31

Halloween

Sunday

I

Boots (detail), *oil on paper*

Monday

2

Tuesday

3

Wednesday

4

Thursday

5

Guy Fawkes Night

Friday

6

Saturday

7

Sunday

8

Remembrance Sunday

Howzatt! 36x48ins, *oil on canvas*

Monday

9

Tuesday

10

Wednesday

11

Thursday

12

Friday

13

Saturday

14

Sunday

15

Padded Up, *sketch*

Monday
16

Tuesday
17

Wednesday
18

Thursday
19

Friday
20

Saturday
21

Sunday
22

Memories 30x40ins, *oil on canvas*, courtesy of John and Pauline Comerford

	Monday **23**
	Tuesday **24**
	Wednesday **25**
	Thursday **26**
	Friday **27**
Saturday **28**	Sunday **29**

My Turn Next 10x8ins, *oil on canvas*

Monday
30
St. Andrew's Day

Tuesday
1

Wednesday
2

Thursday
3

Friday
4

Saturday	Sunday
5	6

County Ground Taunton 10x12ins, *oil on paper*

Monday

7

Tuesday

8

Wednesday

9

Thursday

10

Friday

11

Saturday

12

Sunday

13

The Coach 24x16ins, *oil on canvas*

| Monday |
| 14 |

| Tuesday |
| 15 |

| Wednesday |
| 16 |

| Thursday |
| 17 |

| Friday |
| 18 |

| Saturday | Sunday |
| 19 | 20 |

Tactics 10x16ins, *oil on board*, courtesy of David and Shelly Jones

Monday

21

Shortest Day

Tuesday

22

Wednesday

23

Thursday

24

Christmas Eve

Friday

25

Christmas Day

Saturday

26

Sunday

27

The Christmas Present 10x12ins, *oil on board*

Monday 28
Boxing Day

Tuesday 29

Wednesday 30

Thursday 31
New Year's Eve

Friday 1
New Year's Day

Saturday 2	Sunday 3

Sid Lahiri, Parkside Cricket Academy 16x14ins, *oil on board*

2010

	January	February	March	April	May	June
M		1	1			
Tu		2	2			1
W		3	3			2
Th		4	4	1		3
F	1	5	5	2		4
Sa	2	6	6	3	1	5
Su	3	7	7	4	2	6
M	4	8	8	5	3	7
Tu	5	9	9	6	4	8
W	6	10	10	7	5	9
Th	7	11	11	8	6	10
F	8	12	12	9	7	11
Sa	9	13	13	10	8	12
Su	10	14	14	11	9	13
M	11	15	15	12	10	14
Tu	12	16	16	13	11	15
W	13	17	17	14	12	16
Th	14	18	18	15	13	17
F	15	19	19	16	14	18
Sa	16	20	20	17	15	19
Su	17	21	21	18	16	20
M	18	22	22	19	17	21
Tu	19	23	23	20	18	22
W	20	24	24	21	19	23
Th	21	25	25	22	20	24
F	22	26	26	23	21	25
S	23	27	27	24	22	26
S	24	28	28	25	23	27
M	25		29	26	24	28
Tu	26		30	27	25	29
W	27		31	28	26	30
Th	28			29	27	
F	29			30	28	
Sa	30				29	
Su	31				30	
M					31	
Tu						

2010

July	August	September	October	November	December	
				1		M
				2		Tu
		1		3	1	W
1		2		4	2	Th
2		3	1	5	3	F
3		4	2	6	4	Sa
4	1	5	3	7	5	Su
5	2	6	4	8	6	M
6	3	7	5	9	7	Tu
7	4	8	6	10	8	W
8	5	9	7	11	9	Th
9	6	10	8	12	10	F
10	7	11	9	13	11	Sa
11	8	12	10	14	12	Su
12	9	13	11	15	13	M
13	10	14	12	16	14	Tu
14	11	15	13	17	15	W
15	12	16	14	18	16	Th
16	13	17	15	19	17	F
17	14	18	16	20	18	Sa
18	15	19	17	21	19	Su
19	16	20	18	22	20	M
20	17	21	19	23	21	Tu
21	18	22	20	24	22	W
22	19	23	21	25	23	Th
23	20	24	22	26	24	F
24	21	25	23	27	25	S
25	22	26	24	28	26	S
26	23	27	25	29	27	M
27	24	28	26	30	28	Tu
28	25	29	27		29	W
29	26	30	28		30	Th
30	27		29		31	F
31	28		30			Sa
	29		31			Su
	30					M
	31					Tu

Giclée Prints Available

"Two to Win" Forth Test, Trent Bridge, Ashes 2005
29x40ins, *limited editon of 129 gicée prints*
signed by Ashley Giles, Matthew Hoggard and the artist.

Christina Pierce signing her limited edition prints with *Ashley Giles and Matthew Hoggard* in the Players Dining Room, Edgbaston 2006.

Ashley Giles has bought the original oil painting.

***For further details on all prints, original paintings and commissions contact Christina on tel: 01483 224 721
email: chrissy@christinapierce.com
web: www.christinapierce.com***

OCS Stand at the Oval, 14x36ins

Sachin Tendulkar
12x12ins

Umpire
15x15ins

Brian Lara
24x17.5ins

Waiting to Bat
16x12ins

Matthew Hoggard
24x16ins

The Rose Bowl - County Ground Hampshire
24x36ins or 12x16ins

Huddle
20x24ins

Sachin Tendulkar
18x24ins

Selected from a wide variety of prints available to purchase. Sizes shown are of the image, all prints have borders added.
Prints can be made to other dimensions by request.

Thank You

With love and thanks to my son, Oskar Kolk, for inspiring me, my father, David Pierce, for making Oskar into the cricketer that he is and for all his support.

My mother, Jean Pierce and Joy Brewer for their patience and understanding. Michael Pierce for the logo, Nic Tucker and Chris Bishop for the photography.

Mick Hodson for all the design and production, Sophie Yauner for everything. Val Harris at The Cedar House Gallery, Ripley and Dudley Winterbottom at The Chelsea Arts Club.

Brian Ruby who helped with the selection of information, his expertise with the West Surrey District U10's and all that he has done for Oskar.

Ashley Giles who is a patron and an inspiration, his brother, Andy who coached Oskar at Ripley Cricket Club and who frames my paintings.

Medha Laud at the E.C.B. who has always been brilliant. David English who has helped me throughout and all the counties for supporting this project. Sid Lahiri who is a brilliant coach and David Aylward, Headmaster of Parkside School. Gavin Franklin, the coaches and the U10 Surrey team for all they have achieved this season. Nigel Holman for his help last season.

John Crawley and Nick Pike, Hampshire. Nashy, Middlesex and Jon Robinson at the M.C.C. Cathy and Kevin Sedgbeer at Somerset County Sports, Richard Brice at Somerset County Sports and Bradbury and Mike Burns at Bradbury, for their generosity and belief in me. Rebecca Hough of Dodo Pad for her advice and input.

Nikki, James, Abbey and Georgie Prichard, and Cathy, Gerry, Harry and Sonny Cott for their love and support. Penny and David Hughes, Nikki and Kevin Powell, and Robin and Melissa Copestick for all they have done. David Jones, skipper at Normandy cc for his coaching, knowledge and kindness.

Christina Pierce August 2008

Christina undertakes commissions and also has limited edition prints and origional paintings.
web: www.christinapierce.com   email: chrissy@christinapierce.com
telephone: 01483 224721

Mick undertakes commissions for book design and limited edition prints.
web: www.mickhodson.co.uk   email: mick@mickhodson.co.uk
telephone: 020 8898 1987